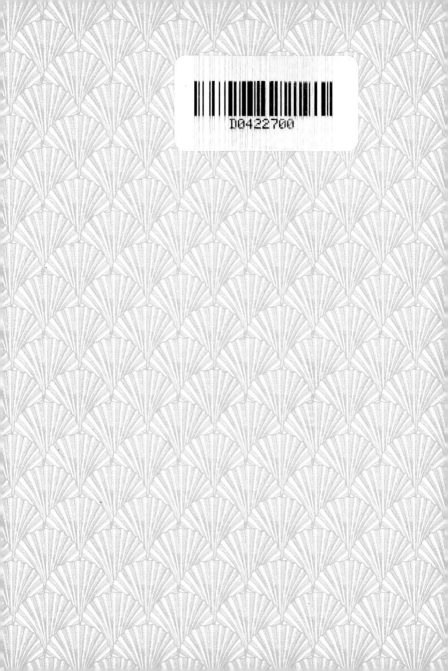

Karen,

See you on "The Waves"

Much Love,

[signature]

9/25/11

SURFING YOUR INNER SEA

way. What I see is a final lesson about serenity, and it has to do with volcanoes.

For decades, centuries even, an active volcano appears anything but. It may hiss or steam from time to time, but most often it's as unmoving as any old mountain. Then suddenly it erupts, with a fury that forever alters the surrounding terrain. The key factor in this phenomenon is that, contrary to all outward impressions, a volcano is never at rest. Far beneath the surface, hidden from view, great transformations are always taking shape.

In many instances, life is just like that. Things aren't going well for us, and no apparent evidence indicates a change. These are times when we grow the most frustrated and discouraged. Serenity feels delusional, like a waste of

SURFING

Your Inner Sea

. . .

ESSENTIAL LESSONS *for* LASTING SERENITY

by RAPHAEL CUSHNIR

photographs by Susie Cushner

CHRONICLE BOOKS

SAN FRANCISCO

Library of Congress Cataloging-in-Publication Data available.
ISBN: 978-0-8118-6728-3

Manufactured in China.

Design by JENNIFER TOLO PIERCE.
This book was typeset in Mrs. Eaves and Bickham Script.

10 9 8 7 6 5 4 3 2 1

Chronicle Books LLC
680 Second Street
San Francisco, CA 94107

www.chroniclebooks.com

FOR AYIN

My fully formless bride

Table of Contents

Introduction

FOR ME, SERENITY WAS NEVER PARTICULARLY APPEALING.
Peace of mind seemed, well, boring. I wanted to grab life
by the horns. I wanted to leap with joy and wail with grief.
I wanted to fight the good fight. I wanted, in the words of
Dylan Thomas, to "rage against the dying of the light."

At the same time, something was clearly missing in my
approach. I grew more and more wrung out and off-kilter
from all that intensity. I knew that it wasn't really sustainable.
So I began to wonder if it was possible to experience outra-
geous passion *and* peace of mind. I read the works of ancient
sages who counseled combining complete involvement with
total detachment. Their ideas spoke to me, but I had no clue
how to put them into practice.

Okay, that's not exactly true. Early on I realized that a
life both exciting and peaceful could only come from looking
within. I explored therapy, meditation, and an eclectic blend
of healing techniques. Still, my inner world remained stormy.
Anything but serene.

Then I discovered surfing. Not the kind with a board
on the ocean, but not that different either. I learned how to

surf my *emotions*, how to ride their wild waves instead of girding against them or getting sucked under. With this new skill came a new kind of serenity, as bracing as it was soothing.

Once I knew how to surf my inner sea, I could then find peace anywhere, anytime, no matter what was happening within or around me. I grew more powerful and successful, while expending less effort. I remained balanced, clear, even when buffeted from one challenge to the next. Amid those very challenges, I also found a way to free my mind, to silence its endless tirades and channel its creative energy.

Not surprisingly, I set out to share my good fortune. I wrote four books. I traveled the world giving lectures and leading workshops. Wherever I went, people always asked, "Which of your books is the best place to start? Is there one that distills the essence of you and your message?"

Until now, there wasn't. That's why I wrote *Surfing Your Inner Sea,* and why I'm so delighted that you've chosen to read it. I view the book as a conversation, a chance for us to sit with one another as if by a warm fire, to feel safe enough that our deepest truths can surface.

I hope the time we spend together will stir you up, fill you with questions, and increase your sense of what's possible. I hope this vibrant vision of serenity is enticing enough for you to experiment with right away.

In my heart, I view that as already happening. I see you thriving at all times, in both calm and blustery waters. I see you uplifted by all tides, flowing with them wherever they lead. I see you, at this moment and ever more, calling forth the greatest possible future through your oneness with whatever comes.

CHAPTER ONE

Acceptance

IT IS WHAT IT IS. UNTIL IT'S NOT. These two simple sentences contain the key to a life of serenity. They describe a truth that's always present, right before our eyes, but that it's often difficult to see.

The foundation of serenity is acceptance. You're already a master of acceptance, even if it doesn't seem that way. You never look at a bird and complain that it's not a dog. You never demand that your kitchen table become a bed. You accept almost everything in your life as it is. You allow each element to take its natural place in the order of things. To argue against this natural order would seem, well, unnatural. It would also make you crazy.

And yet, if you're like the rest of us, there are also many aspects of that same natural order that you don't accept. You don't accept things about your parents or your upbringing. You don't accept things about your work or your colleagues. You don't accept things about the state of the world or its rulers. In response to these affronts, a powerful surge of resistance arises. You insist, "No! It shouldn't be!"

And yet, it is. No amount of proclamation or struggle will ever change that. But still, you fight. Regardless of how much you go along on the outside, the battle still rages within.

Let's be completely clear. Working to make a positive difference regarding any realm of existence is always a great idea. It's part of what makes us human. But real, lasting change always begins with acceptance. If you want to heal a hurtful legacy from your childhood, you must first accept all of that hurt. If you want to improve your job satisfaction, you must first accept whatever makes the job *un*satisfying. If you want to promote social or environmental justice, you must first accept the current injustice.

But beyond just the word itself, or the idea of it, what exactly is acceptance? To arrive at the answer, imagine jumping into a lake. As soon as you hit the water, you realize that the lake is freezing. Instantly, your body recoils, sending the message that this experience is intolerable. Your mind begins screaming urgently: "Get out! Get out! Get out!"

That is the opposite of acceptance.

Now, imagine jumping into a different lake. As soon as you hit the water, it envelops you in delightful, warm waves. Your pores immediately open to soak up all the pleasure. Your mind proclaims a joyful "Yessssss."

That is acceptance—a full mind/body embrace of any experience as if it were a just-right lake.

"Wait a minute!" I can hear you protesting. "How am I supposed to embrace all those lakes of my life that actually *are* freezing?"

Here's how. You say "yes." It doesn't have to be a joyful yes. You don't have to want the experience, or like it at all. It's even okay to wish it were different. In saying yes you simply affirm the one great, unavoidable truth—it is what it is. Then, and only then, can you begin to successfully explore ways to make it different.

I bear the scars of an unhappy childhood—yes.

My boss is rude and unappreciative—yes.

The world is at war—yes. Hunger, disease, and inequality persist—yes. All on a planet that's burning up from poisons of our own making—yes. Absolutely. You bet.

Uh-oh. I can hear you protesting again. "I thought this was a book about serenity. So far all you've done is throw me into a giant funk." This isn't a book about fake serenity, however. It's not about pretending to be serene while ignoring what desperately needs your attention. Instead, the serenity we're after is one that can survive, and even thrive, smack in the middle of even the worst calamity.

The best way to demonstrate the power of acceptance, and its essential role in such real-world serenity, is by sharing a personal story. Many years ago, my first wife had an affair and left me. I was devastated. I couldn't believe that our "perfect marriage," the result of so much conscientious work, could just blow up in a flash like any other union. Every moment of every day felt like immersion into a lake well below freezing.

Rarely did five minutes go by in which my mind didn't pore obsessively over each excruciating detail of this massive indignity. I accepted none of it, not one bit. And I suffered ceaselessly as a result. What made the situation more complex was that my wife actually wanted to come back to our marriage, but didn't know when or how. That left me dumbfounded, paralyzed, trying to figure out if there was actually a marriage left to save, and whether I was even interested.

Should I stay or should I go? This question completely stumped me. I couldn't come close to determining what to do with the marriage itself, because all I really wanted was for things to go back to the way they were before. I longed to make this whole miserable situation disappear. In other words, I wanted a bird to be a dog.

Then one day I just gave up. Something inside me relaxed, unfurled. It is what it is, I realized with resignation. And for the first time I braced myself to experience those frigid waters with virtually no resistance. What happened instead, however, felt like a miracle. The water instantly warmed. I stopped suffering. I didn't like my circumstances any better, but right there in the thick of them I experienced—you guessed it—serenity.

In a way, this was a miracle. It allowed me to move through attempted reconciliations and ultimate divorce with an inner calm I'd never have anticipated. I made the right decisions at the right times, for me, with very little stress or strain.

No matter what type of challenges you face, no matter how impossible they appear to overcome, the first and foremost lesson regarding serenity will work for you the same way it did for me. And here it is: Your greatest suffering comes not from the misfortunes that befall you, but rather from your resistance to them. Therefore, as soon as you fully accept that which seems unacceptable, your pain begins to turn to peace.

• • •

Take the Elevator
Downstairs

YOU CANNOT FULLY ACCEPT ANYTHING about your life that
you haven't yet experienced. You can acknowledge it, or com-
prehend it, yet such semi-acceptance always happens from a
distance. Over there.

True acceptance, on the other hand, is right here. It's
something you feel. Inside. When a wave of acceptance moves
through your body, it's as if every single cell lets go, relaxes,
and surrenders to the ride.

A ride inside. That's not just a description of acceptance, but of virtually all life. Even when objects, events,
and encounters originate outside of us, we still register and
process them within our physical bodies. A ripe red straw-
berry presents itself to your eyes and is promptly decoded
by a delicate array of nerves and neurons. Its smell travels
through your nose in a similar way. Its taste would remain
entirely unknown to you if your tongue weren't likewise
connected to the rest of your flesh.

Many of us, however, relate to our bodies as if they're
apart from us. Over there. Sometimes they're beasts of

burden, existing solely to be used. Other times they're instruments of our pleasure, factories for our brains, or temporary way stations for our souls. To view our physical nature in such ways is to become *disembodied,* to function as talking heads, to retreat into the penthouse of our thoughts while the real stuff of life teems and swirls below.

Here's the second lesson about serenity: it's visceral. To find it, and sustain it, you must venture out of the penthouse and take the elevator downstairs. You must explore your body in a brand new way, and eventually call it home.

Are you protesting yet again? Maybe you're thinking something like, "I hate my body. I'm overweight and uncomfortable. Why would I want to get close to all that?"

Or maybe your response is the opposite: "I *do* know my body. I exercise and take great care of myself."

Either answer, from the standpoint of serenity, misses the point. To illustrate, allow me to share another story. As a freshman at Reed College, in 1977, I signed up for introductory Art History. I was prepared to study Greek urns and impressionistic water lilies. Instead, on the first day of class, my professor rose to the podium and said only this: "In downtown Portland there's a new headquarters building for PG&E. Go look at it. Write a five-page paper. Turn it in next week."

We students begged him for more information and guidance, but none came.

Resistant, anxious, and confused, I headed with my notebook to the edifice in question. I stood across the street, dutifully looked, and drew a blank. What can you write, I thought, about a big block of cement and glass? After a few minutes, however, I noticed a particular design accent between the windows. Then I noticed how the glinting sun brightened an otherwise drab color. Then, the dam broke. I couldn't stop noticing. The building came alive and seemed absolutely compelling. By the end of the day, I had completed my five-page paper with details to spare.

Now what if, instead of a high rise, the assignment had been to write about my direct experience of a pulled muscle, a stomachache, the jitters, or loneliness? What if that were your assignment? Is your body lived in enough to offer five full pages for even the most subtle or fleeting sensation? If so, you're downstairs, indeed.

If not, I invite you to step into the elevator no matter how much you like your body, and no matter what kind of care you take of it. I invite you to listen to your body, not just in fits and starts, but for long, luscious stretches. I invite you to feel the ebb and flow of your sensations, not just when pleasurable or painful, but especially when they're more sub-dued. In doing so, you'll find that serenity is ever-present within, that it's the very space in which your sensations arise and flow.

To some, such sustained attention may seem gruel-ing. But there doesn't have to be anything arduous about it. Instead of approaching bodily awareness like a chore, the way I did with my college assignment, imagine lying down in cool grass and staring up languidly at the sky. Let your physical sensations appear and pass by like clouds. Whatever you notice, accept. Breathe. Notice. Accept.

When you bring the power of acceptance to your internal landscape, when you say yes to your physical body above all else, suddenly right here becomes everywhere. Rather than feeling limited within your skin, or tormented by the aches and pains that reside there, what happens is that the borders of your identity soften and expand. You experience yourself as directly connected to the minutest molecule and the greatest galaxy. The ride is still inside, but now inside contains the whole universe. Literally, in mystical moments, you become what you behold.

CHAPTER THREE

Surf the Waves

IN FIFTH GRADE, OUR TEACHER SHOWED THE CLASS A
Disney documentary about the human body. To demonstrate
how different organ systems functioned, the film featured
tiny cartoon men. These animated characters worked, fought,
and goofed off together. Then, in response to various physical crises, they raced all around the bloodstream in a clamor-
ous panic.

This benign little educational film affected me for
years. It caused me to view my body as a foreign land with
a volatile, at-risk, teeming population. It was my great
responsibility to keep all of these little men safe and well
cared for. On the one hand, this was positive—I certainly
cut down on the junk food. On the other hand, my life
became, with such worried inward attention, a fragile boy-
hood version of *Horton Hears a Who!*

It wasn't until decades later that I gleaned another
aspect of the film's impact. Subtly, unintentionally, it
oriented me to the vast universe within myself. I was "downstairs" whether I wanted to be or not. And even though
I soon realized there weren't actually Technicolor hordes
roaming beneath my ribs, what stuck with me was a sense
of internal perpetual motion. Inside, I knew, everything

was always changing. Even when I was quiet, still, or asleep, my body was still roiling with activity.

A great myth about serenity is that it comes when we slow down. Another is that we best cultivate it during meditation, in candlelight, and at placid locales like ponds and meadows. The truth is, we become the most serene by syncing up with the ever-changing flow of sensation within our own bodies. And it is a flow. Absent the Disney influence, we find ourselves able to detect that flow almost as soon as we seek it out.

I notice there's a rumble in my stomach. Now the rumble intensifies and spreads up my trunk. It stops at my throat, which is suddenly tight. I keep my attention on the tightness in my throat for a bit and then find my cheeks flushed. Tears well. I didn't even know I was sad. Now I do, but still not why.

Rather than searching for an answer, I continue to notice my tears, a few of which roll down my cheek. At the same time I notice that I now feel looser, freer inside. Without intending to, I breathe a deep sigh. And it comes to me then, softly, like a gentle knock at the door. I'm sad because a friend let me down. This effortless recognition brings another sigh.

I keep noticing for a few seconds more, long enough to gather that I'm not really sad any longer. I feel—let's see—peaceful. But I know that if I keep tuning into my inner experience this way, the peacefulness won't remain either. Only the flow will, always, regardless of whether, or how much, I'm aware.

The previous three paragraphs are an example of an ancient practice. I call it "sensation surfing." This simple practice is the fastest way to serenity ever found. It almost always works, no matter how foreign it may seem at first and no matter how much pain, stress, or suffering may be present. It works because it's acceptance in action, performed precisely where needed most.

The practice of sensation surfing is often quite tricky. To understand why, let's look at ocean surfing. Among the most challenging of sports, ocean surfing involves the rare combination of two constantly moving elements. There's the surfer on the board, and also the wave on which she balances. Each millisecond during which surfer and wave proceed in unison, all is well. But at the first instant of disconnect—wipeout.

When sensation surfing, the "wave" is your constantly shifting inner experience. The "surfer" is your attention, following the wave up close, in matching motion. There is absolutely no attempt to control the wave or otherwise alter the experience. It's strictly "Whither thou goest, I shall go."

In this, however, is a wondrous paradox. The very act of surfing your internal waves without trying to change them is precisely what does change them. Your attention facilitates the flow. It creates additional inner space. These two attributes of attention allow turbulent waters to storm freely and calm quickly. They also allow you to keep your balance no matter how enormous the swells.

Imagine—you don't have to get rid of your anger in order to become serene. You can surf your anger *to* serenity. You don't have to get over the loss of a loved one in order to become serene. You can surf your grief to serenity.

Great news, right? And now here's the flip side. Like it or not, you can't get there any other way. If you try to rid yourself of such anger or grief without surfing it, you'll only impede the flow, compress the space. Instead of moving with you, the storm will now rage against you.

The most crucial sensations to surf, therefore, are emotional ones. More feeling, more serenity. Less feeling, less serenity. And that's true across the whole spectrum, from the most pleasurable feelings to the most excruciating.

While it's easy to sign up for such an approach regarding the pleasurable feelings, the excruciating ones are another matter. Wanting to get rid of unpleasant emotions is only natural. What life teaches us, however, is that you can't talk, think, numb, pretend, or deny your way out of them. All you can do, and it bears repeating, is surf your way through them.

With practice, of course, your surfing will improve dramatically. You'll come to enjoy it when least expected, often even before serenity dawns. The most brutal waves, you'll discover with surprise, often provide the greatest ride. Though fearsome from a distance, in the water, in real time, they strengthen your spirit like nothing else.

Still, you're human. Your will, from time to time, will flag. When mine does, I remember that fifth grade cartoon. Everything is constantly changing, it reminds me, especially within. Therefore no experience, even the most seemingly unbearable, must be borne beyond one single moment.

CHAPTER FOUR

You Can't Do It Wrong

AS CHILDREN WE'RE NATURALS AT TRIAL AND ERROR. In learning to walk, we willingly crash to the floor repeatedly. Sometimes we laugh, sometimes we wail, but no matter what we keep trying.

Then, over the years, life beats us up. As a result, we grow tentative. It becomes harder and harder to try new things, and harder still to fail at them. We don't like the way it feels to fail, and therefore invest a lot of protective energy in avoiding the risk.

For some, of course, the opposite is true. These people thrive on risk. But even for them, *emotional* risk is almost always a challenge. Such internal risk-taking requires that we embrace the experience of vulnerability. In combination, failure and vulnerability present a one-two punch that seems unacceptable for even the hardiest of souls.

To ward off this double jeopardy, we develop a mental monitoring function that's almost always on. Relentlessly, it scans our behavior for even the slightest sign of an existing or pending mistake. According to the impossible standards of this self-assessment, we're guilty until proven innocent. If no evidence of wrongdoing is present, the search intensifies.

If evidence does turn up, the berating is immediate, fierce, and nearly paralyzing. Either way, as long as we remain in the throes of this mental monitoring, serenity is a distant dream and successful surfing is an impossibility.

Even for a serene surfer, mental monitoring remains a persistent challenge. When I'm at any social gathering, for example, I automatically become self-conscious and vigilant. "Am I being too reserved? Too outspoken? Excluding this person? Monopolizing that one?" The list of concerns is endless, and this takes place not just with strangers but also with those I know well. Often in such situations I'm drawn to a stiff drink, but I've learned the hard way that alcohol only makes the problem worse.

If such mental monitoring is unavoidable, you might be wondering, then why attempt sensation surfing at all? The good news, in this regard, is that mental monitoring *itself* can be surfed. As soon as you notice that it's rendered you tentative or rigid, turn your attention directly to those sensations and watch what happens. Usually, within just a few moments you'll be back in flow.

For me, at parties, surfing the sensations that result from my mental monitoring is fast, effective, and hangover free. My vigilant monologue becomes a whisper from the next room, no longer preventing me from spontaneous engagement with the other guests.

This approach only works, however, when we're able to witness our mental monitoring rather than fuse with it. All too frequently, we champion a guilty verdict as soon as it's in. Imagine, for instance, that I wasn't a successful surfer at a party. In that case a condemning thought might arise in my mind, such as, "You are too quiet! Say something!" Then, immediately following I'd reflexively second the motion. "That's right! Stop screwing up! Say something already."

If I couldn't bring myself to say something, most likely I'd collapse further inward. And if I did find a way to speak up, most likely it would come across as forced, since it actually *was* forced. As a result, I'd feel worse, not better, and would face a new internal trial for having compounded my original crime. Perhaps the most likely outcome of all is that I would find the first possible excuse to escape the party. Following that, I'd probably turn down a number of future invitations. In other words, I'd flee from the whole painful cycle.

Fleeing is our most common response to a conclusion that we've fallen short of our own expectations. It's why mental monitoring actually causes us to fail more, not less. It's why, for example, we don't stay on diets after slipping. We judge ourselves unworthy to meet our previous goal, and then resign ourselves to lower expectations. Or, if we can't abide such unworthiness, we quickly bounce back, more determined than ever to succeed.

But now are our fists are clenched, our teeth gritted, and such a tense, non-accepting stance dooms our next attempt from the outset. And even if we do beat the odds somehow and meet our original goal, it doesn't provide the lasting satisfaction we previously imagined. We become thin, for example, but miserable.

Fortunately, there's another way. It involves redefining failure as opportunity. Failure, in fact, provides the greatest possible opportunity for growth, healing, accomplishment, and—you guessed it—serenity. How? Failure tells us precisely where we lose the ability to stay present and connected. When we flee from an experience the first time, and then proceed to take advantage of that failure, it allows us to stay exquisitely attentive when we're most at risk the next time. And the next, and the next. Until finally, peacefully, we break through.

What all of this amounts to is that you can't do it wrong. That's because there is no wrong, at least not in this realm. Lest you think this is all just wordplay, let me put it another way. Mental monitoring is what it is. We can't make it into something different, any more than we can make a bird into a dog. Therefore, mental monitoring requires our complete, unfettered acceptance. It's not a problem of any kind. And when mental monitoring attempts to make any part of *us* a problem, that's not a problem either. Instead, it's the best chance for us to hone our no-problem approach to life.

"I can't do it wrong." Say it to yourself softly, again and again. See if you can relax into this realization rather than straining to believe it. See what happens when you permanently let yourself off the hook. For one thing, achieving a lasting sense of serenity will no longer seem so daunting. Now, is *that* something you'll be able to accept?

CHAPTER FIVE

Simple, but Not Easy

I DON'T FEEL SERENE TODAY. I woke up with a bad cold. Every time I cough it makes my head pound. My to-do list is so long that it won't even fit on its usual page. Most of the day's tasks can't be postponed. That means I have hours and hours ahead filled with stress and strain, when all I really want to do is go back to bed and sleep.

Oh, and I forgot to mention the client who's decided not to pay me for her sessions. And the repairman who still hasn't fixed the heater after six visits.

On a day like this, perhaps serenity is too high a goal. Maybe I'd be better off just trying to survive it. Or packing it in and letting all those pressing deadlines pass unmet. Or getting in my car, rolling up all the windows, and wailing at the top of my lungs. At least that might get a little of this pressure off my chest.

I actually had all of the above thoughts about a week ago, while in the bathroom, squeezing toothpaste onto my toothbrush. After they passed, what remained was a sense that sometimes finding serenity requires time, space, and energy, none of which I had on that dreadful day. Trying to be serene, I temporarily concluded, was not only too hard but would actually make things worse.

Many of us make just such a conclusion, and quite often. We assess the external circumstances of our lives as impossible barriers to serenity. No way. Not for me. And especially not now.

Just as often, we assess the internal road to serenity as far too difficult to traverse. Take Jeremy, for example. He lost his family's savings on a bad business deal and felt overwhelmed with shame. I explained to him that sensation surfing could bring him to a place of peace about this misfortune, and he agreed to try. But after a few moments of direct connection with his shame, Jeremy recoiled. "Forget it," he told me. "Too painful. I'll pass on whatever you're selling if it means any more of *that*!"

Whether we gather our evidence from the inside or the outside, the conclusion remains the same—*this serenity business is hard work*. And as much as I'd like to tell you otherwise, I can't. It wouldn't be true. Finding serenity amid internal and external challenges isn't easy. It's simple, yes, but definitely not easy.

This recognition brings us to another vital lesson about serenity—it's a state of being we must earn. We earn it by accepting life's unavoidable difficulties. We earn it by accepting the great pain that those difficulties evoke. Finally, we earn it by keeping our approach to that pain straightforward and direct, not making it any more complicated than necessary.

Simple, but not easy. Nice catchphrase. But let's actually put it to use. Let's start with me. On that sick day last week, I certainly faced many challenges. It's difficult to practice acceptance when congested. I didn't want to say yes to any of it; instead I wanted to say "ick," or "ow," or "enough already!" But right then, after brushing my teeth, I decided to keep it simple and surf. I brought my attention directly to my clogged and draining sinuses. Did it make the cold go away? Absolutely not. But it did create a sense of space, and calm, and allowed me to find serenity *within* my discomfort.

That, in turn, allowed me to face one to-do list task after another with the greatest amount of efficiency and equanimity possible. When I had nothing more to give and really did need to rest, I was able to accept that necessity as well.

Surfing all of the sensations of my cold, as well as the frustration and tension connected with it, also kept my mind from getting bogged down with annoyance about whatever popped into it. Annoyance is like a virus. Resistance is its breeding ground. Soon the virus reaches epidemic proportions and virtually everything ticks us off. Acceptance, on the other hand, stops such an epidemic cold. Though the facts of any given situation may remain the same—non-paying client, incompetent repairman—they lose their infectious power.

Now what about Jeremy and his overwhelming shame? He did keep it simple. He sensation surfed the emotion exactly as I asked, yet wiped out almost immediately. Jeremy didn't need to be told, "You can't do it wrong," because he hadn't fallen prey to mental monitoring. Nor had he neglected to turn failure into opportunity. It wasn't himself that he judged a failure, but rather the very process I'm advocating.

In light of all that, I invited Jeremy to give it one more try, only this time to take the ride incrementally. I suggested that he stop connecting with the shame whenever it began to seem too painful, and to resume only when a sense of peace, balance, and ease had returned. I let him know that we had plenty of time, and that he could stop and start as often as necessary.

Jeremy agreed. It turned out that he needed about an hour of intermittent connection to experience a complete emotional shift. The shame didn't depart completely, but it went from what he called a twelve, on a scale of one to ten, all the way down to a four. Grateful that he stayed with it, Jeremy now understood from his own experience that "not easy" doesn't mean impossible. What it does mean, in the words of Robert Frost, is that "the best way out is always through."

• • •

CHAPTER SIX

Befriend Your Nemesis

WE'RE DEEP IN THE WOODS, SURROUNDED BY FALLING SNOW, safe and warm at a rustic retreat center. Seated on the floor in the traditional workshop circle, thirty participants have bonded together in their mutual search for lasting healing and happiness. Refreshed from the previous exercise, they smile, laugh, and revel in their newfound powers of acceptance.

Now, it's time for me to break this reverie. I ask the participants to think of their nemesis, that person back home who makes everything uncomfortable, difficult, and contentious. Choose the person, I advise, without whom life would be so much easier. As you can probably guess, most people identify their nemesis instantly. The room fills with knowing chuckles, but also with palpable tension. Just the mention of these peace-disturbers brings up so much frustration and resistance.

Next, I ask the participants to zero in on the most objectionable quality or behavior of their nemesis. Once that's complete, I ask them to discern the way that this objectionable quality or behavior makes them feel. I instruct them to let their answers go beyond frustration and resistance. Picture, I tell them, having to endure the impact of this nemesis while wide open and defenseless.

Then, we go around the circle and each participant names an emotion that arose. The list includes *rage, fear, hopelessness, unworthiness, powerlessness, guilt, shame, impatience, humiliation, grief, despair, jealousy, resentment,* and *abandonment.* Finally, I ask the participants if the emotion they shared is particularly difficult for them to engage. Everyone nods.

This experience repeats itself in virtually all workshops I facilitate. It points toward a simple shift in perception that can make a world of difference. Rather than viewing our nemeses as problems, we instead can see them as golden opportunities. Why? Because the emotions that they elicit provide the greatest serenity training.

Imagine—That boss for whom nothing is ever good enough starts up his usual harangue, but this time you're able to listen to it without reacting. Instead, you remain present, accepting, and peaceful.

Imagine—That rude and misbehaving child acts out like always, but this time your blood doesn't boil. Instead, you're able to assess the situation clearly and then take appropriate action, regardless of the response that ensues.

All that's necessary for such serene scenarios to occur is your willingness to surf what seem to be the most dangerous waves. Surf any nemesis-provoked emotion three times, either during or directly after an encounter, and it will lose almost all of its ability to knock you off balance.

Notice that I specified that the surfing could occur during or after an encounter. That's because it might not be appropriate in your corporation to cry tears of humiliation during a staff meeting. It also might not be helpful to tremble with rage in the presence of your teenager. But if surfing isn't called for in the moment, there's always later. And later works just as well, because those waves don't dissipate with time.

Actually, they intensify. This intensification requires some explaining, especially for those who question the need to surf the hard feelings that a nemesis provokes. Indeed, at first glance, other approaches to such people may seem much more attractive. You might be drawn to avoid them, "suck it up," or go on the offensive.

Sometimes, temporarily, one of those approaches helps you get by. But what about that original emotional wave? Where does it go? The answer, alas, is that it doesn't go anywhere. An unsurfed wave remains within. But its mission is to get out. And one way or another, it's determined to fulfill that mission. So each time you refuse it, the wave just comes back stronger.

If you continue to match a wave's intensity in your effort to keep it at bay, much of your available life energy gets siphoned off in the process. You become stressed, depleted, and ultimately depressed. Our international epidemic of depression can be viewed, in part, as a widespread reluctance to surf. While many depressed people deal with a bona fide chemical imbalance, many others choose medication over feeling. While this choice can often be a lifesaver, especially during periods of great trauma, it can never obliterate the initial wave.

An unsurfed emotion drops beneath your awareness. It becomes part of your unconscious. Once there, in order to get your attention, it draws people and situations into your life who will elicit the same wave. By deciding to avoid or gird against a current nemesis, you literally guarantee the appearance of another one in the future. Different face, different situation, same feeling.

What about going on the offensive? Wouldn't seeking a change in the behavior of your nemesis be a proactive way to address the problem, both now and in the future? Yes, but only if you've already accepted everything about the nemesis. Trying to change a person's behavior without first accepting its impact hinders your ability to perceive and pursue the best possible course of action. The pressure cooker inside continues to steam, clouding your vision ever more.

Surf first. Always. Once "on shore," you'll find clarity and creativity much easier to come by.

But that's not even the greatest gift. What comes from surfing first is a realization that there is no nemesis. There is no person you must evade or defeat in order to remain safe and serene. No one stands in the way of your ultimate fulfillment.

Therefore, there's another way to describe this gift. It's called freedom.

CHAPTER SEVEN

Mental Aikido

YOU ARE NOT RESPONSIBLE FOR YOUR THOUGHTS.

There, I said it. And with those seven words I may have just saved you from a lifetime of guilt, worry, and regret.

Of course, I'm not expecting you to believe me just because I said so. Instead, let's look at the evidence. Picture yourself in the produce section of a supermarket, rolling a cart past some jumbo pears. A thought crosses your mind.

"Last time I saw pears that huge was on Uncle Dave's farm." Then, another thought. "Too bad he and Aunt Sue split up." Then another. "I can't believe she's going after his retirement accounts." And another. "She's the greediest person I've ever met."

Now, picture yourself on the freeway. Someone cuts you off and almost causes an accident. At the very same moment that you register the driver's appearance, you also fall prey to a silent outburst: "Learn how to drive, you fat pig!"

Finally, picture any recent time that you came down hard on *yourself.* Recall the negative "tapes" that played in your head. They probably enumerated all the ways you fell short of your expectations, as well as everything else that's supposedly wrong with you.

What links these three examples is that all of the thoughts in them arose unbidden, of their own accord. You couldn't have stopped them no matter how hard you tried. Even more important, you didn't consciously create them. It's not as if you set up shop in your brain, piecing together molecules and firing synapses to create the questionable finished product.

You're not responsible for your thoughts. Now does the idea make more sense? It refers to the vast majority of what goes through your mind. There are, of course, other types of thoughts that you definitely do will into existence. These include the ones that appear when you're creative or solving problems. But such intentional thoughts don't usually cause guilt, worry, and regret. And even in this intentional realm, many of your most important thoughts arise when you're *not* trying to think them. They happen in the shower, or in dreams, or at other times when your conscious mind is on hiatus or occupied elsewhere.

"An idea just popped into my head." See—even our language reflects the way thoughts are usually independent of us thinkers.

Why is this realization so essential to serenity? Because as soon as any thought arises in our minds that we don't like or approve of, we reflexively fight back and lose whatever serenity we previously possessed. How do we fight back? With other, contrary thoughts.

For instance, the criticism of Aunt Sue might immediately lead to a round of self-flagellation: "Why'd I think that?! What's wrong with me? She's always been so kind and generous." The outburst at the driver might be followed by: "My God, how could I be so judgmental? I mean I'm just as fat." And at the first notice of negative tapes: "Stop it! Right now! You'll never amount to anything while you're so hard on yourself."

Sometimes, we don't have the will to fight back. Instead, we stoke the fires of negativity until we're totally inflamed. About Aunt Sue and her ilk: "Some people only care about money. If I ever get married, it's with a prenup for sure." About fat people: "They're so selfish. We oughta force 'em to drop the pounds." About ourselves: "What's the use? I'll always be a total loser."

You're not responsible for your thoughts, especially the negative ones. Okay, then, what are you responsible for? You're responsible for how you respond to thoughts once they arise. The truth is, neither fighting back nor fanning flames will ever benefit the world around you or within you. In the aftermath of negative thoughts, there's only one thing that will. Acceptance. Just as with feelings, however, most of us want to *do* something about these thoughts rather than let them be. Yet, letting them be, as you're about to see, is nowhere near as passive as it seems.

In the martial art of aikido, the practitioner doesn't fight directly against an opponent. Instead, the practitioner channels the opponent's own energy to gain an advantage and remain safe. Mental aikido works much the same way. Rather than doing battle with a negative thought, you disarm it completely with an overwhelming barrage of acceptance.

Say a negative thought crops up in your mind. Approximated by words, this would be your internal stance: "Welcome! Thanks for coming. Stay as long as you like. Take up all the space you need."

A negative thought simply cannot survive in that environment. It's looking for a fight, or at least an easy target. Without any tension to feed off, the thought simply disappears whence it came.

Plus, there's even better news. Unlike an emotion, which requires a period of surfing in order to depart, a welcomed thought vanishes instantly. On this you have my guarantee. The thought may surface again periodically, but each time it does mental aikido will work just as well.

Soon, after consistent use of this technique, your internal environment will no longer breed such thoughts. You'll also come to see that most negative thoughts are projected by repressed emotions. In the calm that mental aikido fosters, you'll be much better able to spot and surf those emotions quickly.

Together, sensation surfing and mental aikido are powerful enough to bring peace and perspective to even the most troubling times. I'd call them the perfect one-two punch, except that doesn't quite sound serene.

· · ·

CHAPTER EIGHT

The Compulsion Cure

FOR A BRIEF SPELL DURING MY TWENTIES, I lived in a tiny second-floor studio just up the street from Venice Beach, California. While the famous boardwalk usually teemed with people below me, I was often alone, far from friends and making little headway as a screenwriter.

On Friday and Saturday nights, my loneliness was particularly intense. I felt it as an ache of dislocation in my gut. This wasn't where I was supposed to be. This wasn't what was supposed to be happening. It was wrong. I was wrong.

My internal ache projected itself onto the scenery around me. The apartment's funky woodwork, which at other times looked bohemian and celebratory, now came across as tawdry and pathetic. The rough beams, set at haphazard angles, seemed to reflect the mess I'd made of my Hollywood dreams. I wasn't a hip, sought-after boy wonder. Instead I was a desperate also-ran, no different from a million others, trying to paint over my emptiness with fame.

And, on top of all that, I couldn't get a date.

Needless to say, I didn't know how to sensation surf. The idea of mental aikido would have sounded like gibberish. Plus, my body couldn't handle liquor or drugs. All I had at

my disposal was a beat up little TV and Häagen-Dazs. So I'd lower the shades, find a mindless show, and spoon my way into a sugar coma.

I got by this way, week after week, except that my love handles ballooned and so did the ache.

What are your compulsions? Are they related to food, like mine was at the beach? Or, perhaps your coma of choice has to do with sex, shopping, e-mail, or something else from the endless list. No matter your preference, it's impossible to blend compulsion with serenity. A compulsion allows you to resist your experience, temporarily, while serenity calls for acceptance. A compulsion puts you to sleep, even if not literally, while serenity requires your full and complete presence.

This means that to increase your serenity you must decrease your compulsions. That's easier said than done, of course, but it's also nowhere near as hard as it seems.

Are you skeptical? Are you ready to put my assertion to the test? To begin, let's zero in on exactly what happens during the compulsive cycle. The cycle initiates when a challenging emotion arises. Most of the time you're unaware of this experience. Your unconscious, however, is already moving to quash it. It selects one of your compulsions and presents you with a conscious desire to go for it.

Along with that desire comes an overall "itch," a sense of discomfort that can only be relieved by satisfying the compulsion. If you can't take immediate action, however, even just the commitment to do so as soon as possible will provide a sufficient, short-term reprieve. Once you do satisfy your compulsion, this overwhelms the original discomfort with either a rush of adrenalin, or a blanket of numbness, or both in that order.

At some point in the future, as the benefit fades, you're likely to feel guilty or shameful for giving in. But soon afterward, the cycle is bound to repeat, only this time with more intensity on the front end and less satisfaction on the back end. In other words, every compulsion loses a little of its intended effect with each go-round. You're left, as a result, with a stronger, though still unconscious, version of the original emotion. The conscious itch toward fulfillment grows nearly unbearable, even though there's an equally conscious recognition that such fulfillment is an illusion.

There's one key point, amid all this grasping, when the cycle is especially susceptible to successful intervention. That's when you first notice the itch. This itch, as you might already guess, can be surfed. And all the panicky thoughts that arise along with it can be welcomed into submission with mental aikido.

If you're willing to experiment with this approach when your next compulsion is afoot, you'll find that everything about the itch intensifies. Bigger wave, harsher thoughts.

But then, if you can stay with it, the itch departs. In its place arises the challenging emotion that began the whole cycle, only now it's conscious.

In its conscious state, this emotion can be surfed like any other. And after you surf a number of these waves, your system gets the message that feeling this emotion directly is a safer, healthier, and overall better strategy than compulsion. As a result, the compulsion wanes. It won't return, either, as long as you continue to surf.

It may take a while, however, before you make much headway. *Accept, accept—you can't do it wrong.* Each time you're unable to handle the itch, notice exactly what sensation or thought sent you racing back to your compulsion.

Aware now of what caused your greatest difficulty, you'll be better able to handle it next time. Soon you'll make it past the itch and all the way to the underlying emotion. Here, too, there may be many times early on when you can't handle the intensity. Here, too, *you can't do it wrong.*

Remember the Serenity Prayer—*God grant me the serenity to accept the things I cannot change; courage to change the things I can; and wisdom to know the difference.* The key to benefiting most from this powerful prayer is recognizing that what you can change changes moment by moment. That's why *you can't do it wrong.* That's what sensation surfing and mental aikido are all about.

Lasting change can only be secured incrementally. Each moment that you accept a little more, you change a little more. Even, paradoxically, when you accept the current limits of your acceptance.

A compulsion, therefore, can best be understood as a question: "Right now, in this moment, what do I need to accept?" The cure for compulsion, not surprisingly, comes from your acceptance of the answer.

CHAPTER NINE

The Order of Things

YOU'RE A LIZARD, BASKING IN THE SUN. ALL IS WELL. Then
a cloud crosses the sun. Is it about to rain? Should you dart
off your rock and into the brambles? Then the sun comes
out again. You pause, consider: Can the warmth and light be
trusted? Seems so, and you relax again.

But, now, you're hungry. What to eat? There's a scuttle
on the other side of the rock. Is it lunch? You inch closer,
closer, and then pounce. Midair, you realize your mistake.
What looked a harmless insect turns out to be a scorpion.
It's too late to retreat. At the moment your claws touch stone,
the scorpion strikes. At the same time, you fling your scaly
body sideways. The stinger glances your hide but doesn't pene-
trate. You race to safety down a nearby crevice.

That lizard I described actually lives inside you, all
the time, in the form of what neuroscientists call your reptilian brain. This part of your brain, the first to develop along
the evolutionary path toward *Homo sapiens,* is binary in nature.
At all times, it's assessing your current situation along the
continuum of safe/dangerous, as well as the continuum of
like/dislike.

Life, obviously, is much richer than that. It requires
a subtler response to the vast array of experience that's always

coming your way. So now, you're a mood ring. Depending on exactly what's happening at any moment, your color changes to match it. There are the basic, primary hues—blue, red, green, yellow—that signal a shift in actual "mood." But on top of that, you can display a million subtle shades to reflect each and every nuance of personal reaction.

Of course, no actual mood ring is that fine-tuned, but your emotions are. The part of your brain that creates most emotions is the limbic system. Developed second in the course of your brain's evolution, the limbic system produces emotions with wide-ranging differences of intensity. It also combines emotions, each with its own degree of intensity, so that your overall emotional response to any given situation is potentially unique.

It's certainly helpful to have a keen response mechanism to life's inevitable ups and downs. Such a mechanism adds a gratifying dimension to your ongoing assessment of safe/dangerous and like/dislike. But what are you then supposed to *do* with all of this information?

Well, now, you're a full-fledged human being. You can ask why, discern data, find patterns within data, devise solutions to the problems presented by data, imagine reality beyond data, and even create additional meaning and resonance to this whole abstract process by means of artistic expression.

All of the above activity occurs primarily in your neo-cortex, the third and final region of your brain's evolutionary development. This "triune" structure of your brain, and the order of its historical creation, was first hypothesized by Paul MacClean. His model points out that the brain's three layers are arranged in a hierarchy of complexity, with the neo-cortex more complex than the limbic system, and the limbic system more complex than the reptilian brain.

Yet the model also specifies that no one layer of the brain is superior to the other. For a complete brain to function optimally, each of its layers must work not just at full capacity individually, but also in harmonious partnership with one another.

Whenever this happens, so does serenity. And since serenity occurs so rarely for most of us, it follows that the three layers of our brains aren't usually such good partners. We're already on track to make them so, however, with our commitment to acceptance. We're even closer whenever we perform sensation surfing and mental aikido. The last thing we need to do is to apply the wisdom of evolution, in real time, to each occurrence of disharmony.

In other words, when serenity eludes us we must attend to ourselves in the same order of the brain's evolutionary development. If the reptilian brain goes on high alert, the limbic system bogs down. At that point, even if we're willing, it becomes impossible to feel. Likewise, if we haven't yet felt all of the emotions produced by our limbic system, the advanced functioning of the neocortex is for naught. Even if it seems that we're abstracting our way to well-being, such emotion-deprived analysis ends up making things worse, not better.

Analysis before emotion fuels compulsion. It's almost always a disguised attempt to *get rid of* feelings, and in the end it only leads to ornate, extravagant castles of denial. They're often as deadly as they are beautiful, which is, in part, why the previous century of human history, with all of its amazing intellectual breakthroughs, has brought us to the brink of destruction.

Stepping back from that brink will require our entire species to feel before thinking and to think before acting. It will also require us to recognize that a reptilian high alert, with no actual danger nearby, means difficult feelings are present within us. This point is crucial. The reptilian brain possesses a drastic flaw. It mistakenly responds the same way to an unpleasant emotion as it does to footsteps in a dark alley. And as long as it perceives any kind of threat, whether internal or external, it will refuse to cooperate fully with the brain's other two layers.

The main signs of high alert are rapid heartbeat, shallow breathing, sweaty palms, and heightened tension. They may occur alone or in any combination. Whenever they do, your one and only job is to surf. Greet the symptoms of high alert as you would any other physical sensation. If you're not in actual danger, such gentle, patient attention always causes a quick "stand down." Afterward, full emotional flow can then resume, followed by truly beneficial reasoning.

When this reordering of attention comes to pass with regularity, for the majority of earth's population, we will have embarked upon a brand new stage of evolution. The triune brain, you might say, will have evolved into a holy trinity.

CHAPTER TEN

Stress Test

I CAN'T WAIT ANY LONGER. IT'S THE ELEPHANT IN THE ROOM. In a book about serenity it would be irresponsible of me to write another word before dealing directly with stress. Nothing prevents serenity more than stress, or kills it off more quickly.

But what, exactly, is stress? The truth is, the experts don't agree. They part ways in describing exactly what causes it and what happens to us once it occurs. What they agree upon is the difference between good stress, like the kind you use to strengthen muscles while lifting weights, and bad stress, like the kind that's involuntary and diminishes your ability to function. They also agree that different people are stressed by different things, at different degrees, and at different times.

My wife likes roller coasters, while even just the thought of one stresses me out. A pressing deadline gets my creative juices flowing, while she freezes up as soon as the clock starts ticking.

There's one type of stress, however, that seems to tran- scend such personal and subjective differences. This is the stress resulting from a discrepancy between the demands of a situation and our presumed ability to meet them. In other words, what we're called upon to do is just too much. When this happens, our reptilian brain goes into high alert and stays

there. As long as neither we nor the demands placed upon us change, no amount of sensation surfing, mental aikido or evolutionary reordering will reduce our stress for a significant degree of time.

Did you notice how in the previous paragraph I used the word *presumed*? It may be you or someone else who does the presuming. For now, let's stick with you. Your presumption is almost always about the limits of your own capability. For instance, "I can't do ten things at once. Or, there's no way I can finish this report on time." But are such assessments actually true? And how do you find out for sure?

One way to begin is by separating what you believe from what you know. Ask yourself, "Have I been in this situation before and truly tested my limits? If so, have there been any changes in my life or skill set since then that may have increased my capability?"

You can't, of course, answer such questions while in high alert. Such deliberateness at that point would amount to meditating in a burning house. But if you surf your way to even just a few moments of calm amid the stress, a reliable answer will come. If it does, and you realize that the jury is still out on your capability, then you can return to the task at hand as an experiment. Whether you succeed or fail, you'll gain valuable information. And when the doubting thoughts resurface, "I can't. . . . I can't. . . .," your deftness with mental aikido will keep them sufficiently at bay.

Another way to discern the truth about your capability in a stressful situation is to home in on the way it makes you feel. Apart from your capacity to perform the desired task, are you capable of tolerating the actual experience of stress it produces? To be more specific, now that you've become at least an advanced beginner in sensation surfing, has your new skill allowed you to handle stress better? If so, that's another reason to return to the task at hand as an information-gathering exercise.

The previous two approaches are about stretching your limits. A third approach involves the possibility of *over*stretching. This often occurs when we hold ourselves to a higher personal standard than is possible to reach. We think we *should* be able to do something, but the truth is we can't. Here, stress arises not so much from the demands of the situation itself as from the unrealistic pressure we bring to it. Whenever you suspect this may be true in your case, ask yourself, "Would I take on this task with no 'shoulds' involved? What if it were equally acceptable not to complete it?"

Okay, enough about you. Even if you weren't push-ing yourself too little, or too much, contemporary society is a stress-producing machine. All but the most fortunate among us must work too long and too hard just to make ends meet. Plus, we're constantly coerced to consume above our means and then must work even more to pay for it. It's not just about work or consumption either. We've fallen prey to a trance of frenzy. With all of technology's timesaving breakthroughs, we're busier than ever before. Busyness itself is a compulsion. Stillness is viewed as practically immoral. Nothing in the evolution of our species has prepared us for this challenge. We're simply not made for the lives we lead.

In spite of all that, however, serenity is still possible. In order to remain serene amid stress-crazy times, you must learn and remember one more lesson: No matter how overloaded you are, no matter how demanding your situation, you can do only one thing at a time. And that one thing, for its one moment, is all you need to do.

Sometimes, the one thing you need to do is determine what you need to stop doing. After asking all of the questions above, you come to realize that the demands placed upon you are indeed too much. But once you've sorted that out, and even while you're sorting it out, you still only need to do one thing at a time.

Once you internalize this lesson, you can then fully give your all to the call of each moment. Whatever it asks of you will always be possible. Whatever the outcome, you'll always know you did your best. Undistracted by the past or future, unswayed by the demands of other moments, you'll finally be free. And that freedom will reveal capabilities within yourself that you never previously dared to desire.

What is stress? Just as with compulsion, it's a question. And this time the question is—what needs to happen next?

CHAPTER ELEVEN

Fairy Matching

THE JAPANESE ARE WIZARDS AT SERENITY. Think of the tea ceremony and Zen gardens. What these placid products of Japan have in common is a high degree of order. Every element fits in its perfect place, and doing so harmonizes with every other element. There's lots of space, too. The sips of tea come with such deliberateness that each moment of repose, before and after, feels as important as the activity itself. The rake creates its graceful sand patterns as if following invisible, previously etched grooves.

All of this serenity is critical for the Japanese because the rest of their society is so frenetic. They live crammed together on teeming islands. Their cities overwhelm the senses with a neon-drenched cacophony. You might say that the meditative aspects of Japan are an attempt to bring balance to a lifestyle that would otherwise be totally *out* of balance. And this raises the question—what would a lifestyle look like that was serene by its very nature?

In contrast to Japan's extremes, consider the long, steady life of a redwood tree. A redwood can live for more than 2,000 years and grow to almost 400 feet tall. With leaves high above the forest floor, it's relatively impervious to the otherwise deadly ravages of insects, fire, and flood. It just grows and grows, serenely, a little at a time over a long stretch of time.

Yet, a redwood tree is profoundly limited in its adaptive capacity. It can only live on one small stretch of earth. It can only produce one type of leaf and grow in only one direction. If its environment becomes inhospitable, a redwood is literally stuck in the mud, unable to pick up and travel to friendlier surroundings. Therefore, while inspiring to behold, this mighty tree doesn't offer us much instruction for serene survival amid today's fast, furious, unprecedented change.

But my niece does. Beatrix is about to turn seven, and she's an ace at the card game Concentration. She doesn't play with the usual deck. Instead, she uses one that features pairs of fairies. There are flower fairies, midnight fairies, river fairies—twenty duos in all. Beatrix calls this game Fairy Matching, and she beats me at it every time.

With uncanny accuracy, Beatrix keeps track of which fairy goes with which. She doesn't just remember but also intuits. You may think I'm deluded by pride, but I swear it's true: I've seen Beatrix successfully select four sets of fairies in a row without ever having seen them turned over beforehand.

How does she do it? I'm not sure. But clearly, she has an uncanny knack for knowing what belongs together, and also when. She doesn't just turn on this suprarational skill haphazardly. She saves it for those rare moments when I seem to be mounting a challenge, when I might for once actually win.

Now what can Beatrix's fairy matching teach us about serenity? The same thing, more or less, that was taught by Ecclesiastes. "There is a time for every purpose under heaven." Remember, in the last chapter, when I suggested that in each moment there's only one thing you need to do? I described how understanding this principle allows you to heed each moment's call. What I haven't yet described is exactly *how* the call comes. Most of the time, it's through energy.

Energy, the kind of subtle, intuitive flow I'm referring to, is a controversial subject prone to lots of grandiose claims and confusion. Yet every one of us has a "sixth sense" and has felt it countless times. Whether we heeded it is another matter. Beatrix heeds her sixth sense continuously because she hasn't yet been talked out of it.

Heeding your own sixth sense in relation to the call of the moment means recognizing whatever energy is present. While there are endless types of energy, most of us encounter just a handful each day. There's to-do list energy, for instance, when suddenly you notice an increased ability to "take care of business." There's also communication energy, when suddenly it's right to talk things over. In addition there's contemplation energy, playful energy, and even housecleaning energy.

When we align ourselves with the energy of the moment, our capacity to thrive increases by leaps and bounds. When we disregard that energy, and try to accomplish something out of sync, it becomes as difficult as it is unpleasant.

I bet you already know this. Haven't you forced yourself to clean house at least once when housecleaning energy was nowhere to be found? The chores were grueling and seemingly endless, right? But how about when you cleaned house with the recognition that "Now is the time to clean!"? Didn't everything go quickly and smoothly, as if the wind were at your back?

Every once in a while, the demands of everyday life make it impossible to match our actions with the energies we perceive. Our kids suddenly need us when it's time to relax, for example. Or, we get a clear message to nurture ourselves right before a big work deadline. At those times, tuning in, we realize that the wind can't be at our sails, and that resisting that truth would only amount to misreading the *entirety* of the moment.

More often, though, we don't actually have to mis-align with the energy that's present but do so anyway because it doesn't fit our plans. We try to impose our will on the moment, in spite of our sixth sense, due to plain old stub-bornness. We want what we want when we want it. And the cost of that stubbornness is—by now it should be obvious—our serenity.

Every moment, fortunately, provides a new opportu-nity to get that serenity back. The fastest, most efficient way is to tune in, and then match that moment's specific purpose under heaven. Once you do, it's not just wind that appears at your back. Sometimes it's also fairies.

CHAPTER TWELVE

The Right People

THE MORE SERENE YOU BECOME, THE EASIER IT IS to spot serenity's absence. In particular, you grow increasingly able to recognize the people in your life who don't jell with or support your newfound peace of mind. Which brings up the obvious question—what are you supposed to *do* with those people?

This question first plagued me regarding Mary, my childhood best friend. From the age of six till twenty, we were nearly inseparable. Our connection survived through an array of shifting interests and cliques, as well as the hormonal storms of adolescence. Each of us challenged one another, as Mary was deeply intuitive and I, not yet having taken the elevator downstairs, was colossally cerebral. We also counted on one another's solace and support through the inevitable catastrophes of growing up. I hugged away her tears after she forgot the words to one of her first choral solos, while she helped me run away from home for a day to take a stand against unfair punishment.

Yet, from the very beginning, there were also seeds of discord between us. Mary was so charismatic and popular that people were constantly lining up to do her favors, with no

reciprocation expected or offered. She grew used to that, but I never did. Plus I was massively in love with her, and that wasn't reciprocated either. As the cocoon of our school years came to an end, I emerged to question everything about life and my unbalanced friendship with Mary above all.

One day, I put my needs on the table with almost mathematical precision. "If our friendship is going to work for both of us," I told her, "you have to call me back the first time I leave a message, not the fourth or fifth." Alas, I was the only person holding her to such a standard, so she responded to my plea with defensiveness and a clear lack of enthusiasm. I'm also sure, to round out the picture, that over a decade of pent-up frustration warped my communication to a stammering, off-putting degree.

When the dust cleared, however, I stuck to my guns. I called once, she didn't call back, and that was the end of our friendship. Overdue for this change, I didn't grieve much or obsess about it. In fact, I eagerly sought out new, more balanced friendships and found some soon afterward.

It happens that way often. Following serenity's lead, we shed the "skin" of dissonant relationships with a surprising lack of drama. In fact, self-created drama and serenity are entirely incompatible. Even when old mental messages tell us the show must go on, we can no longer find any motivation.

Leaving the scene, however, isn't the only choice. Earlier, you'll recall, I wrote about the demise of my first marriage and how accepting it allowed me to heal. What I haven't yet shared is that for many years afterward Lynda and I remained true soul mates, and, without question, the closest person in each other's lives. For me, there were great gains from this closeness. First, I wasn't yet ready to let go. Second, Lynda understood me like no one ever had before. Third, her personal and professional brilliance were always inspirational to me.

When it came to Lynda, accepting all of those gifts meant also accepting the chaos with which they came. At that point in her life, she was erratic, confused, addicted, and unable to tell the truth in any consistent or reliable way. As long as I kept trying to turn that bird into a dog, my acceptance flagged and I suffered as a result. But the more I owned my choice—"She is who she is, unless or until she changes"— the more clarity and tranquility I experienced. None of this made her ethical lapses right in my book, and I continued to make my feelings known about them. But what I didn't do was gird myself against them and become brittle as a result.

Then, one day, it *was* time to leave. As a result of my serenity, I didn't have to think about it at all. I just knew it from the inside out. Without needing Lynda to change one iota, and with nothing but love in my heart, I simply and silently moved on.

Almost for certain, you have your own versions of Mary and Lynda. Take a moment to reflect: "To best foster my deepening serenity, what relationships no longer serve me? And what relationships call for a recommitment of my acceptance, as well as a willingness to move on when all I've accepted no longer fits who I've become?"

It's likely that your reflection will yield quick, intuitive answers. It's just as likely that those answers will be immediately followed by a stream of thoughts and emotions all about why you couldn't possibly heed them. If not, go forth and prosper. If so, remember that the only things in your way are thoughts and emotions. That means that you already have the tools at your disposal—sensation surfing and mental aikido—to move through them with relative ease.

Impatience, however, stands out among all other emotions as a special threat to the serene overhaul of your relationships. If you become too eager for such overhauls, there's a good chance you'll shoehorn them into inopportune moments when the energy isn't quite right. Your impatience will therefore make everything more difficult and awkward, leading to pain on all sides that's entirely avoidable.

Remember how optimal times exist for play and house-cleaning? The same is true for relationship realignment. If you're having a hard time waiting for the right time to end a relationship, or to redefine it, do your best to surf that impatience rather than acting upon it impulsively. "Waiting," as the great sage Tom Petty once wrote, "is the hardest part."

Yet often, when you surf that waiting wave to wherever it leads, the people there to greet you are the right ones after all.

CHAPTER THIRTEEN

Stumbling Blocks

ONE WAY TO UNDERSTAND THE MESSAGE OF THIS BOOK is that serenity is ever present, always yours for the taking, so long as you can identify and clear out what's in the way. We've already explored many of the things typically in your way—compulsions, stress, other people—so now it's time to focus on the structure of your everyday life.

Speaking of structure, picture the layout of your living room. Is there a clear path from one piece of furniture to the other (apart from temporary stacks of laundry, of course)? How about the path from the living room to the other rooms of your home—are those clear, too? Most likely the answer is yes, or else you'd be unnecessarily tripping over things all of the time. And if something were consistently in the way, you'd soon realize it and move the object.

All of that is obvious, for the most part, and nothing more than common sense. But many of us lose that thread of common sense when it comes to the structure of our usual activities. We make plans and fall into habits that become stumbling blocks in the way of our serenity. We trip over these stumbling blocks constantly, painfully, rarely asking ourselves if the lives we've built could stand a little remodeling.

That's because we're attached to the structures of our lives the way they are. Letting go of those structures requires, well, letting go, and over time we've become awfully comfortable with those stumbling blocks, even while cursing them simultaneously.

Every morning, for example, I used to spend about forty-five minutes reading the newspaper. It tired me out, depressed me, made me feel like I needed a break before the day had even begun. But I couldn't part with this routine for what seemed like totally valid reasons. First, the morning paper had been a part of my life for decades and felt literally a part of me. Next, I was passionately interested in the world and had no faster way of keeping up with the endless rush of current events. Finally, it *looked* like a relaxing activity, at least whenever I saw someone else doing it in the movies or on TV, and I couldn't yet accept that it just wasn't that way for me.

But then came the Internet age, and I began exploring my news-gathering options online. I found that I could fulfill my news fix in about fifteen minutes. This made me less depressed, targeted my attention more efficiently, and gave me a crucial half hour at the beginning of the day when I needed it most. To be fair, that also meant letting go of my old ritual, as well as the opportunity to stumble upon those quirky items of interest that routinely fill a newspaper's pages. I was more than happy to make the trade-off, however, because it so clearly removed a major stumbling block to my serenity.

Yet the Internet, as you'll now see, also *created* another stumbling block. Here's how I found out. Last week I was leading a retreat and presented the participants with an automatic writing exercise. I asked them to start writing with a phrase I provided, and to not lift their pens off the page for fifteen minutes. This type of writing allows the unconscious to seep into our awareness, and helps us access the deepest possible truth in any situation. The phrase I asked the group to begin with was, *My biggest self-created obstacles to serenity are . . .* Once I rang the chime for the exercise to begin, I decided to perform it myself. Here's a portion of what came through.

I notice I have a habit of checking my e-mail about twice as much as necessary. It seems to come from a belief that I must stay on top of things at all times or an emergency will arise that I won't be able to handle. Beneath this belief lies a fear, I'm sensing, that allowing myself to feel fully serene will come back to haunt me, that it isn't really safe.

Yeah, this feels true, even though I'm the Serenity Guy! Well, we teach what we need to learn, right? And everyone needs a serenity tune-up from time to time.

So—I need to surf that fear whenever it shows up. And to practice mental aikido with my related beliefs. Beyond that—how about?—I could—

maybe no e-mail for a couple of hours each morning, afternoon, and evening. Gone fishing. All but my serenity can wait. Yikes. Feels like taking on too much. I better start slower than that. Treat this like a compulsion. Expand into any possible discomfort gradually. What'd be a good starting point? Hmm. My intuition tells me thirty minutes.

Breathing, breathing, checking the intuition. Uh-huh—definitely feels right. Y'know if this works, ideally, I'd be able to close my e-mail program when not in use, rather than always keeping it on. Wow, that'd be great. Serenity would come before vigilance, instead of the other way around. Come to think of it, I bet I'd handle my e-mails a lot more efficiently, too. And while I still wouldn't put off till tomorrow what needs to be done today, I'd also become better able at

putting off till tomorrow what really ought *to be put off till tomorrow.*
Oh, shoot, time's up. Where did I leave my chime?

Now it's your turn. Are you willing? Whenever the time and energy are right, set a timer for fifteen minutes. Grab a notebook and pen. Don't stop writing, no matter how awkward it may feel, and no matter how much your internal editor tries to butt in, until the time is up.

My biggest self-created obstacles to serenity are . . .

I found the chime. I'm ringing it now. Begin with the phrase above. Write away!

· · ·

CHAPTER FOURTEEN

Curiouser and Curiouser

ON THE SECOND DAY OF MY RETREATS, I often ask the participants to share something particularly vulnerable about themselves that they usually keep private. This strengthens the bond between them, and also increases the amount of healing and transformation possible.

You and I have been together for thirteen chapters now, so it's probably a good idea that I share in the same way. Okay . . . well . . . this isn't so easy. There's something I want you to know that isn't very attractive. You might even judge me for it, or perhaps view me a little suspiciously. But it's all for the best, right? So . . . I'm going to take a deep breath and proceed.

Ever since I was little, I've been a bit of a know-it-all. I sometimes think I've got all of the information, as well as all of the answers, even when nothing could be further from the truth. At the age of fifteen, for example, I refused to celebrate our nation's bicentennial. I knew exactly what was wrong with this country. So I spent that July 4th straddling the diving board of my suburban backyard pool, hunched over my journal, writing a lengthy letter to Thomas Jefferson about all of the ways we'd destroyed his democratic dream.

That's right—no sparklers, no firecrackers—just a withering critique that reeked of arrogant, snotty, adolescent grandiosity. But wait, it got even worse. When I was twenty, not yet even of legal age, I told friends that I'd pretty much figured life out. I predicted that my basic values and perspectives would remain the same from that point forward. What a schmuck! I was lucky those friends didn't laugh me out of town.

If you haven't yet lost all faith in me, perhaps I can now lend some nuance to the tale. Because, obnoxiousness aside, I wasn't completely wrong. Many of my values and perspectives have remained virtually unchanged from their late teenage form. If you knew me at twenty, you wouldn't be shocked to meet me today. Later, when life broke me open, it didn't swap out my essential personality. Instead, it perforated the one already present. I became, at least I'm told, a softer, more accessible version of myself. I learned to meet the world not with certainty, but with curiosity.

Entrenched beliefs are the enemy of serenity, while curiosity is its great ally. Remember the old saying, "Would you rather be right, or happy?" During my cocksure days, I chose "right" just about all the time. What I gained in smugness, I lost in peace. And I didn't win many people over to my point of view, either.

In the background, as I write this, I can hear my twenty-year-old self protesting vehemently. "What are you talking about?! How can you say I'm not curious? I read everything I can get my hands on." He's right about that, no doubt, but there's a key distinction he doesn't grasp. We can seek information either to buttress our current understanding or to expand it. In the buttressing version, we soon petrify with resistance; while in the expansive version, we cultivate flexibility. Along with that flexibility comes the willingness to grow in whatever direction our discoveries point us, even if that means leaving behind what we once supposedly knew for sure.

The title of this chapter, "Curiouser and Curiouser," is a quote from *Alice's Adventures in Wonderland,* spoken by Alice when confronting conditions through the looking glass. In truth, from the vantage point of serenity, life is equally wild and unpredictable on both sides of the mirror. Curiosity, therefore, never leads to righteousness, rarely leads to clarity, sometimes leads to wisdom, and most often leads to wonder.

Wonder, too, is a great ally of serenity. It allows us to remain wide-eyed and receptive, to see birds for birds and dogs for dogs, no matter how curious things get.

Uh-oh. As soon as I finished that last sentence, my twenty-year-old began hollering again. "I'm not an idiot. I know all that! I read *The Wisdom of Insecurity* in high school.

Zen and the Art of Motorcycle Maintenance, too. You're not more spiritual than me—just more complacent."

Okay, here's where it gets tricky. Have you ever known anyone who spouts a party line but doesn't seem harmonious with its message? He's like that—the twenty-year-old—smart enough to swallow the idea of serenity but still unable to digest it.

Are you a little like that, too, perhaps? Is there any part of your serenity talk that you're as of yet unable to walk?

Remember, it's okay. You can't do it wrong. In fact, recognizing what lives uneasily within you, and becoming curious about it, is the quickest way to nurture its ease. *He* doesn't know that. Or if he does, he just won't go there. Instead he chooses to cling to his outrage.

"That's right. You got it." (He's back again. Let's hear him out.) "Just like the bumper sticker says, 'If you're not outraged, you're not paying attention.'"

Once again, he does have a point. Sometimes I *can* get complacent. And on this side of the looking glass, there's definitely room for outrage. What we do to one another and the rest of the planet is a travesty, obviously ripe for massive change. But the essence of serene living is to let wonder and outrage march arm in arm. Too much wonder makes us woozy. Too much outrage makes us strident. What keeps them in delicate balance, above all, is curiosity.

Every once in a while, I'd be remiss to leave out, our genuine curiosity ends up confirming rather than upending what we thought previously. When this happens, though, our perspective doesn't harden—it deepens. We discover new dimensions within our existing understanding, and stay curious about them, too. I may still be a bit of a know-it-all, for example, but nowadays all of the facets of that interest me, draw me in. I actually get excited, rather than defensive, whenever the subject comes up. The truth is, I guess, that I want to know all about it.

CHAPTER FIFTEEN

Name That Attunement

IMAGINE THAT YOU'RE A SCREENWRITER, toiling for years on film scripts that never get produced. Your chosen form of creativity is a blueprint for a finished work of art, but not an actual work of art itself. Therefore, the first time a film that you've written comes out is cause for wild celebration. To see your own name onscreen, finally, makes all that wrestling with the blank page worthwhile.

That moment was about to dawn for me in the early nineties. But then, on a technicality, my credit was denied. Not by some nefarious studio but by the very union pledged to protect writers. I was crestfallen. Furious. Hoping for some peace amid the injustice, for a natural high of sorts, I scheduled the first available appointment with my acupuncturist.

The acupuncturist responded to my tale of woe with quiet compassion. Next she said, "Whenever I have a lot of anger, I go to a shooting range and vent it with a thirty-eight."

Say what?

In addition to reassessing whether I wanted this particular human being to be poking needles into my skin, I knew instantly that her suggestion was about the last possible thing I would ever do. I'd never shot guns in my life. I supported their strict control. I was committed to nonviolence. All of which made me realize, upon a little further reflection, that this particular form of anger management was something I absolutely had to try.

Soon afterward, vowing to make the most out of this sojourn beyond my comfort zone, I headed off to the nearest range. I received a brief course on gun handling and safety, and was then left on my own with a gleaming, lethal weapon.

I took aim. I fired. I imagined blowing away all those who had caused me to lose my precious credit. For a few moments, it seemed to be working. Anger surged. A little piece of it left my body with every bullet. But then the manager walked by, took a look at my target, and pronounced that I was an uncanny marksman. While it was true that I'd hit one bull's-eye after another, his comment ruined my experience. From that point forward, I couldn't help but focus on my accuracy. The bull's-eyes continued, but the anger took a predictable back seat.

Undaunted, I decided to come back the next day for another try. This time, my protective headgear malfunctioned. I did get out a good deal of anger, but I also lost hearing in one ear for the next three days.

During those three days, my rage gave way to classic Jewish guilt. I viewed this loss of hearing as punishment by God, or at least by fate, for abandoning my values so cavalierly. "How dare I take up weapons," I wailed inwardly. "I *deserve* to be smitten. I shall wear this deafness like a scarlet letter."

Once my hearing returned, I quickly forgot all about such biblical hyperbole. My remaining anger stayed mostly stuffed. Other than a funny story, I didn't gain much from the experience till much later. With time I came to see how it demonstrated a key principle of serenity—attunement.

Remember how, in Chapter Eleven, I suggested matching the energy of each moment with the activity best suited for it? In a similar way, the energies *within us* have their own "wavelengths." To deal with them effectively, and serenely, we must first attune ourselves to these wavelengths. If we attempt to respond to inner energy without such attunement, we only roil the waters. Waves of all lengths, and from all directions, inevitably clash. Surfing to serenity becomes impossible.

In truth, there are only seven main wavelengths in the human range of energy. They include:

1) *Survival energy,* which emanates from the base of the spine

2) *Primal energy,* both sexual and emotional, which emanates from the lower belly

3) *Intuitive energy,* also known as "gut feeling," which emanates from the solar plexus

4) *Loving energy,* which emanates from the area of the heart

5) *Communicative energy,* which emanates from the throat

6) *Mental energy,* which emanates from between the eyes

7) *Spiritual energy,* which emanates from the crown of the head.

Attuning to these wavelengths means surfing them, as usual, but with an added eye toward what type of wave you're riding. You can make a quick assessment by simply noticing where in your body the wave is centered. Attunement also means discerning the needs of the situation from the perspective of that particular energy. Besides your attention, in other words, what else does the wave need in order to subside completely?

Take my show biz anger, for example. Decades later, I can still access a trace of it just below my navel. Clearly, it was primal. But back then I didn't relate to it primally. Instead, I related to it mentally, falling in love with an *idea* about what it needed rather than relying on a direct assessment. As a result, I pitted one type of energy against another and bumbled forward unsuccessfully.

It might seem, upon first consideration, that attunement would lead to reacting out of a "lower" energy rather than a more enlightened one. In fact the opposite is true. Attunement allows you either to handle the energy completely, at its source, or to reach a more serene state of being that is optimal for determining the best possible additional action.

Most likely, had I attuned to my primal anger, it would have eschewed a firing range for some far simpler means of expression—perhaps a long, fearsome scream. Or two or three or four. My guess is that such screams would have provided a quick, efficient, complete way through my turmoil. Plus, undoubtedly, both of my ears would have been able to hear them.

• • •

CHAPTER SIXTEEN

Sexpression

SEX IS CREATION . . . LIFE . . . DESIRE . . . ECSTASY . . . DEATH. No wonder it rattles us so, and generates such challenging waves to surf. The more we resist it, the more it consumes us. American sexuality is a perfect example, with its toxic tug-of-war between repression and obsession.

Yet let's be clear—sex is just an energy, a wavelength like all others. When we look at sex through the clear lens of acceptance, it provides less trouble and more opportunity. Because sex is such a powerful energy, it crashes against our blocks and therefore illuminates them better than anything else.

Earlier in my life, I was filled with urgent sexuality like most other young males. But I couldn't get most objects of my lust to return the favor. This was connected to a block about receiving love, although I didn't know it till much later. What I did know was that it felt like one long, painful implosion. The pain assaulted me on every level, primarily emotional, and eventually grew debilitating enough for me to seek counseling.

Marilyn, a practitioner of the Voice Dialogue technique, met my angst with profound acceptance. Once, after striking out at a party filled with great prospects, I whined to her about those "James Dean guys" who leaned against the wall and

exuded irresistible sexuality without even doing anything. What was wrong with *me*? Why couldn't I ever do that?

Hearing my questions, Marilyn calmly asked me one in return. "Would you like to meet your own inner James Dean?" The suggestion filled me with doubt, terror, and intrigue. I gulped, and asked her to lead the way. She guided me to change seats in the office so that I could more easily imagine shifting into this previously concealed part of my personality.

What Marilyn did next, at she explained later, was attune to the sensual energy within her. Then she let that energy enter the gaze between us, which instantly ignited mine. This sudden surge of sensuality between Marilyn and me felt alien, awkward, and somehow totally natural all at once. Over time I felt more and more like I really was James Dean, not the actual person but the symbol and what it stood for. Marilyn and I remained silent, still, just looking, for another few minutes.

Gently, Marilyn retracted her sensual energy while still maintaining eye contact. I felt her withdrawal and responded in kind.

"This 'James Dean' self belongs to you," Marilyn said softly. "It's as much a vital part of you as your arms and legs. The choice of its expression is also up to you, regardless of how others respond."

Marilyn gave me permission, plain and simple, to let my sexuality breathe. All I needed after that was a real-life counterpart. This took another year, after which I was on my way.

Eventually, I traveled the entire distance from imploding adolescent to keynote speaker on the topic of Sacred Sexuality. And my message whenever I speak on the topic is, in essence, the same one in this book.

When you grasp at any outcome, especially your own pleasure, it's impossible to surf the wave right beneath you. And when you resist that wave in any way, a wipeout is guaranteed. Applied to sexuality, that leads to two fundamental points.

First, no sexual thought, desire, or feeling can ever be wrong. Once it arises, it just is, like any other bird. Take a moment to revel in the freedom and flow of that. Imagine the state of the world, tied up in perpetual sexual knots, if we all stopped judging sexual energy and began surfing it instead.

Now I bet that before you were able to invest much imagination in this exercise, an internal moral voice boomed forth: "Sexual energy is not always okay. There is abuse. There are predators. We can't sanction people's perversions and make everything 'all good.' That kind of relativism leads to evil, whether you want to admit it or not!"

Remember, none of this has to do with approval of actions, but only with the acceptance of energy. Accepted energy leads to serenity, freedom of choice, and greater compassion and wisdom. Resisted energy leads to an *increase* of the very energy we seek to counteract. This increase, in turn, makes it more difficult to prevent harmful actions.

The second fundamental point regarding sexuality deals with the act of sex itself. While the sexual revolution of the sixties and seventies promoted positive attitudes about pleasure and the body, it also, unintentionally, made sex more goal-oriented. People enthusiastically expanded their repertoire of sexual positions, fantasies, erogenous zones, and orgasms. As a result, many began to focus on the shore, or the *getting*, rather than on the wave of the moment.

Focusing on the wave of the moment, sexually, is both a simple and a radical act, even more revolutionary than anything our culture has yet seen. It means joining in sexual partnership with nowhere to go and nothing in particular to experience. It means letting the wave take *you*.

Sometimes that leads to sexual fulfillment beyond your imagining. Sometimes it leads to no sex at all, and the revelation that uncleared emotions stand in your way. Sometimes it adds a surprising new spiritual dimension to your encounters, which, even more surprising, intensifies physical pleasure rather than overriding it.

No matter what happens, however, keep letting go of the need to control your sexual energy. Instead, rededicate yourself to attunement, trusting and reveling in the expression that results. Soon, you'll no longer need to fight your urges, to endlessly negotiate your needs. You'll come to consummate, with every trembling cell in your body, the union between wild and serene.

CHAPTER SEVENTEEN

Cockroach Wisdom

TOWARD THE END OF THE EIGHTIES, my body stopped working. After what seemed like an ordinary bout of the flu, I never fully recovered. For many hours each day I was beset by staggering fatigue. My previously iron stomach, for no apparent reason, became an unpredictable minefield.

Searching for an explanation, I went to the doctor. And then another doctor. And then another. Over and over, I heard the same verdict—there's nothing wrong with you. But clearly there *was* something wrong with me, psycho-somatic or otherwise, and I needed guidance in how to address it. This need sent me on a deluxe tour of complementary medicine, from its well-respected center to the diciest of its fringes.

Wherever I went, a new culprit for my malady was revealed. Sometimes it was a virus, such as Epstein-Barr. Other times it was a syndrome, like Leaky Gut. Most often it was labeled an "imbalance." Usually there was a test administered to prove the imbalance, and this seeming clarity would always uplift me. But then my spirits would just as quickly plummet, as soon as the recommended treatment provided absolutely no relief.

After months on this medical sojourn, with symptoms still as mysterious as they were unrelenting, I withdrew. No more doctors, mainstream or alternative. No more prescriptions, pharmaceutical or herbal. I vowed to get to the bottom of the mystery myself, and began by the process of elimination. Everything that might be stressing my system had to go, starting with the likeliest suspects. That meant alcohol, sugar, wheat, dairy—pretty much all the good stuff. When that didn't help, I began avoiding possibly noxious environments. The mall, for instance, was suspect for its sensory overload. Even air and water were off-limits, unless sufficiently filtered.

Soon I grew brittle and high-strung. Waiters were quickly annoyed at my endless questions—"How was it cooked? Was there something else on the grill? Any pre-packaged sauces?" I stuck to my conviction, however, and gained support from others in the same predicament. We saw ourselves as canaries in a coal mine, as early warning systems of a world befouled.

While certainly understandable, the way I dealt with this medical crisis in its first years didn't increase my wellness or earn me much serenity. What I gained in control, I lost in freedom. This is similar to the way many people approach their own challenges, and not just those about illness. First they identify threats to their peace of mind—"I can't be around my mother." "Politics depress me." "My spirit just sinks in a big city." Then they plot their retreat. Which isn't wrong, to be sure, but it always comes at a price.

And that brings us to the lowly cockroach. A cockroach may hide, but it never retreats. The cockroach's motto is "Adapt!" It finds ways to survive, to thrive even, in just about any environment. Remember the old adage that cockroaches will be the only species to make it through nuclear war? I don't know if it's true, and I certainly won't be around to find out, but just the possibility is instructive.

Uneasy with my self-imposed moratorium on everything, I began to think about the schooling a cockroach might impart. I imagined it would look up at me with with pity, but at the same time wag its antennae as if to say, "You oughta know better." And then, the real sermon would begin.

"The opposite of serene, you silly human, is finicky. What good is well-being in a sterile bubble? I mean c'mon, I'd rather swig Raid. If you're so good at surfing your emotions, why can't you do the same with the outside world? Don't demonize that cheeseburger; evolve a new stomach for it. Don't flee from that toxic waste; light your house with its glow!"

As you can see, cockroach wisdom only goes so far. Had I cavalierly pursued many of the things that caused me the most systemic stress, my condition surely would have deteriorated. Likewise, if all of us sought to do a million years of evolving in one lifetime, we'd quickly perish.

Still, over the years that followed, I took the gist of cockroach wisdom to heart. While accepting the limitations

I'd been dealt, I also kept testing and updating them. In other words, if sugar made my symptoms worse in February, I downed a small bite of cake in March. Sometimes I was met with a setback, and sometimes I was freed to indulge. Sometimes I had to update in backwards fashion, meaning that a new license to dig in would later get revoked. No matter what, however, the whole experiment was always worthwhile. It allowed me a life at the edge of my capacity, rather than one needlessly diminished.

I realized that just as serenity doesn't require any particular pace, it doesn't prefer a monastery either. Or a cave. Or anything else that sets us apart from our surroundings.

What it does require, on the other hand, is a commitment to the same kind of testing and updating I've just described. This is similar to two practices we discussed earlier: matching our activities to the energy of each moment, and consciously attuning to our inner energies. In this case, the idea is to walk an ever-shifting bridge between self-care and flexibility, between shaping our environment and adjusting to it.

If we succumb to the tempests around us, and don't consistently seek the greatest possible shelter in each moment, there's no question that our serenity will fade. But if we don't keep updating our requirements for well-being, and don't learn to live as well as possible *within* the tempests, we'll never find the eye of any storm.

Today, my fatigue persists. So does my shaky stomach. No cause has ever been identified and every day offers me new inner and outer waves to surf. While riding those waves, I never stop wishing for better health. But I never get out of the water either.

• • •

CHAPTER EIGHTEEN

Volcano Time

IN BRINGING THESE REFLECTIONS TO A CLOSE, I'd like to share three brief stories. The first one is about a client of mine named Michelle. When Michelle first contacted me, her marriage was in a shambles and it was clearly time for divorce. Yet, she couldn't even bring herself to separate. Her paralysis was sustained by guilt and fear. The guilt stemmed from her role in the marriage's downward spiral, from what the breakup would mean for her kids, and from the idea that jumping ship just wasn't acceptable. Her fear stemmed from never having been on her own, financially or otherwise.

Michelle and I worked together for almost two years before anything changed. Throughout, she condemned herself for inaction and remained hopeless about a break-through. During this time, I counseled that patience and timing were everything, and insisted that where she saw only inertia I perceived tremendous healing.

Then, one day, Michelle moved out and filed for divorce. No fanfare led up to it, no drama accompanied it, and no second-guessing followed it. Her momentous decision, in the actual doing, felt as ordinary as a walk around the block.

The next story is about my early days as a writer. When I was only nineteen, my very first screenplay was almost produced. After that I kept writing screenplays but got nowhere. The feedback was usually positive but came with a hitch. "Great characters, but not commercial enough." "Great story, but no role for a star."

At such a young age, I wasn't yet able to handle the overwhelming waves of hurt, anger, grief, doubt, and shame that accompanied my inability to make it. Throughout most of my twenties these waves kept growing in size and intensity, mostly because I foolishly tried to beat them back.

The worst of it came when I took a job linking celebrities with political causes. During the campaign for an environmental initiative known as Proposition 65, I worked with some of Hollywood's biggest stars. We often shared the same barnstorming bus, and I felt as if my nose was pressed against fame's glass, so close and yet still denied. "You don't get it," I wanted to scream. "I'm not really an advance man—I'm one of you!" In truth, however, I wasn't, and the sting of it was too much to bear.

Soon after the election, I nursed my sorrows and drained my savings on a long trip through Latin America. Almost immediately after I got home, an offer came for more political work with celebrities. Broke or not, I just couldn't do it. I said no, without any idea how to make ends meet.

Then the next day I got a call, out of the blue, to rewrite a film script for real money. I instantly worried that it was a hoax, or a fluke. But the gig was real. It led to another one that was even better, and a decent show biz run over the years that followed.

The third story is about my lifelong quest for a family. Ever since I can remember, I've had a way with kids. We speak the same language, and seem to bring out the best in one another. From the age of thirteen to twenty-five, almost every paying job I had was with kids—teacher, tutor, coach, camp counselor, playground director. Having kids of my own seemed inevitable, and as natural as breathing. For a brief spell in my early twenties, I even considered adopting a child as a single parent.

Then my life took many unexpected turns, and left me entirely without children. The older I got, the less likely it seemed a family would be in the cards. I didn't stop trying, however, and even went so far as to screen every potential date for her own interest in kids. Still, what once seemed like the path of least resistance now felt like an artificial push.

Then, for unrelated reasons, I moved to a different state. Within six months I was co-raising a five-year-old, and, within another year, I had a beautiful daughter of my own.

On the surface it may seem that these stories are about good things coming to those who wait, or about the importance of holding onto our dreams. But I don't see them that time even to contemplate. And indeed, if we lose touch with the depths, if we give in to despair, our future serenity *will* become less likely.

Yet none of that has to happen. To prevent it, we must sync ourselves to volcano time. Whenever it seems like the tide is flowing backward, or endlessly stagnating, we must stay afloat, facing forward, mindful that mysterious and powerful forces are simultaneously at work beneath us.

Then, when the eventual eruption occurs, we're ready, nimble, positioned to ride out the hazards, and to reap all the rewards. Here, amid careening molten lava, we grasp one last benefit from all our practice with emotional waves. For it's now abundantly clear, to our perpetual amazement and delight, that we're equally adept at surfing fire.